SPOTLIGHT ON NATIVE AMERICANS

PUEBLO

Linda Buellis

PowerKiDS
press.

New York

Published in 2016 by The Rosen Publishing Group, Inc.
29 East 21st Street, New York, NY 10010

First Edition

Editor: Sarah Machajewski
Book Design: Samantha DeMartin
Material reviewed by: Donald A. Grinde, Jr., Professor of Transnational/American Studies at the State University of New York at Buffalo.

Photo Credits: Cover, p. 13 (right) Nativestock.com/Marilyn Angel Wynn/The Image Bank/Getty Images; p. 5 Wolfgang Kaehler/LightRocket/Getty Images; pp. 6–7 DEA PICTURE LIBRARY/De Agostini/Getty Images; p. 9 Nagel Photography/Shutterstock.com; p. 10 Duncan Gilbert/ Shutterstock.com; p. 13 (left) Werner Forman/Universal Images Group/Getty Images; p. 14 Fototeca Storica Nazionale./Hulton Archive/Getty Images; pp. 15, 25 UniversalImagesGroup/Universal Images Group/Getty Images; p. 17 National Park Service/Wikimedia Commons; p. 18 John Cancalosi/ Photolibrary/Getty Images; p. 19 Underwood & Underwood Publishers/Wikimedia Commons; p. 21 Chris Maddaloni/CQ-Roll Call Group/Getty Images; p. 23 courtesy of Library of Congress; p. 26 The Denver Post/Denver Post/Getty Images; p. 27 Chris Felver/Archive Photos/Getty Images; pp. 28, 29 Joseph Sohn/Shutterstock.com.

Library of Congress Cataloging-in-Publication Data

Buellis, Linda.
 Pueblo / Linda Buellis.
    pages cm. — (Spotlight on Native Americans)
 Includes index.
 ISBN 978-1-5081-4120-4 (pbk.)
 ISBN 978-1-5081-4130-3 (6 pack)
 ISBN 978-1-5081-4122-8 (library binding)
 1. Pueblo Indians—History—Juvenile literature. 2. Pueblo Indians—Social life and customs—Juvenile literature. I. Title.
 E99.P9B85 3026
 978.9004'974—dc23
                           2015029391

Manufactured in the United States of America

CPSIA Compliance Information: Batch #BW16PK: For Further Information contact Rosen Publishing, New York, New York at 1-800-237-9932

CONTENTS

WHO ARE THE PUEBLO PEOPLE?

CHAPTER 1

Thousands of years ago, North America was occupied only by Native Americans. Their **ancestors** made their home in present-day North America long before Europeans arrived. Today, there are more than 500 Native American groups in the United States and more than 600 in Canada.

Many Native American communities are located in the southwestern United States. Known collectively as the Pueblo people, they come from communities such as the Taos, Acoma, Zuni, and Hopi. These nations are ecocentric, which means their ways of life have been shaped by the **environment** in which they live. Because of this, each nation's **culture** is different.

Historically, Native Americans faced many challenges to their traditional ways of life. Europeans, especially the Spanish, brought change that threatened the Pueblo people's survival. However, the Pueblo people's ability to adapt allowed them to survive in a changing world, while their respect for the past has helped preserve their **heritage**.

People of Pueblo descent honor their culture by wearing traditional clothing and performing traditional dances and ceremonies.

MIGRATING TO A NEW LAND

CHAPTER 2

Although the Pueblo people may have been in the southwestern United States far longer than people of European descent, their ancestors were not from North America originally. One theory is that ancestors of Native Americans came from eastern Asia. Their **migrations** may have occurred during an ice age, which is a period of time marked by very cold temperatures.

According to this theory, sea levels were much lower during the ice age than they are today because much of the water was frozen in great ice sheets. That means places that are covered by water today were once dry. Historians think this was the case with the land between northeastern Asia and Alaska. This area is thought of as a land bridge, or a connection between landmasses. Ancestors of Native Americans may have walked between Asia and North America using this land bridge.

Scientists aren't sure when these migrations took place, but it was more than 12,000 years ago. Over time, the water levels rose, covering the land bridge. Asia and North America were separated by the sea. Ancestors of Native Americans could no longer go back—they could only go forward.

There are many theories about how ancestors of Native Americans came to live in North America. Some scholars feel the best way to describe this time in history is to think of it as people coming from Asia, the Pacific Islands, Africa, and Europe, and blending together before Europeans arrived.

REACHING MESA VERDE

CHAPTER 3

Around 10,000 years ago, migrating people moved south through North America. Earth's climate warmed and became similar to the conditions we have today. Moving around the continent in small groups, the first peoples were hunters and gatherers. This means they hunted wild animals and collected plants to survive. These groups spread out and lost contact with each other. They developed separate cultures and lifestyles based on their environment. That's why Pueblo communities that formed in the area that's today Arizona may have been different than those that formed in the area that's today New Mexico.

Historians say Pueblo culture began during the Late Basketmaker II **era**, which was almost 2,000 years ago. During this era, ancestors of the Pueblo people changed their lifestyle. They became farmers and grew squash and maize, or corn. Historians call them Basketmakers because they were skilled at making baskets of woven plant materials.

About 1,400 years ago, ancestors of some Pueblo people settled in the region that's today the southwestern United States. They're known as Ancestral Puebloans.

They chose to settle in a place called Mesa Verde. This name means "green table" in Spanish. People here farmed and made tools that were more advanced than their ancestors' tools. These developments allowed small groups to grow into large villages. Soon, their population reached in the thousands.

Mesa Verde National Park in Colorado contains almost 5,000 known archaeological sites related to Ancestral Puebloans. Their village-like settlements led to the name "Puebloans," which means "village dwellers" in Spanish.

PIT DWELLERS, CLIFF DWELLERS

CHAPTER 4

Ancestral Puebloans lived in pit houses from about AD 100 to AD 750. The pit houses were built a few feet into the ground. They were often built into the top of a mesa, or flat-topped hill, or in the spaces between cliffs. Pit houses contained a fire pit and a hole called a sipapu, which—as you'll read later—had special meaning to the Ancestral Puebloans' **origin story**.

Ancestral Puebloans started building structures above ground around 750. Houses were built against each other in rows that followed the curve of the cliff they were built under. By 1000, Ancestral Puebloans were building these structures to have two or three floors with more than 50 rooms. The outside walls were made of sandstone bricks, which were held together by a mix of mud and water.

Some of these dwellings contained a partly underground room called a kiva. "Kiva" is a Hopi word for a round or rectangular room used in traditional ceremonies. It was entered by a ladder from the roof. Ancestral Puebloans had great kivas that were used by the whole community, while kivas inside houses were used by individual families.

Ancestral Puebloans used materials available in their environment to create their homes. They created sandstone bricks by cutting sandstone with harder stones that were found in riverbeds, and used a mixture of mud and water to hold the bricks in place. The houses themselves were built into the side of a cliff, which was part of the area's geography. Ancestors of Pueblo peoples who lived in other areas may have built homes that were better suited to their specific environment.

THE CLASSIC PERIOD
CHAPTER 5

The years 1100 to 1300 are considered the Classic Period for the Ancestral Puebloans. Their dwellings housed thousands of people. Clans, or related families, likely lived together. They made tools from resources in their environment, such as bone, wood, and stone. They were accomplished builders and successful farmers. Some Ancestral Puebloans were artisans, which means they created goods and crafts. These people were skilled at weaving and jewelry making. However, they may be best known for their pottery skills.

Ancestral Puebloans started making pottery when they settled in communities, and some of the **techniques** that developed during the Classic Period are still used today. Pueblo pottery included pots, bowls, mugs, **canteens**, and more. Pottery, which was made by women, was used for everyday needs as well as in traditional ceremonies.

Pueblo pottery is considered one of the most highly developed Native American art forms. Potters make their works by hand, rolling long coils of clay and piling them into the shape of their pot. Once constructed, they smooth the inside and outside, decorate it, and fire it to make it hard. Pueblo pottery commonly features **geometric** designs with flower, animal, or bird patterns.

Anthropologists use the design on pottery to trace the development of Pueblo culture. Changes in design elements can help anthropologists determine when and where it was made, as well as which community made it. Here, you can see the differences in this pot from around 1100 and the pottery created in modern times by these Zuni women.

EASTERN AND WESTERN

CHAPTER 6

Ancestral Puebloans abandoned their cliff dwellings in the Mesa Verde region around 1285. Anthropologists think the Pueblo people may have left because changes in the climate made it difficult to farm.

Ancestral Puebloans migrated south into present-day Arizona and New Mexico. By the 1400s, Pueblo people were living near the Rio Grande, the Zuni River in New Mexico, and the Hopi mesas in Arizona.

The Pueblo people are split into two groups: the Western Pueblos and the Eastern Pueblos. Western Pueblo communities include the Hopi, Zuni, Acoma, and Laguna. Western Puebloans had a matrilineal society, which means their family history was traced through the mother's side. Eastern Pueblo communities include groups

Hopi Pueblo community

such as the Taos Indians. For these communities, family history was traced through both the mother's and father's sides.

The food used by these groups differed based on where they lived. Western Puebloans hunted animals such as rabbits and gathered wild plants. Eastern Puebloans grew maize along the Rio Grande. Men hunted deer and antelope, and sometimes they traveled to the Great Plains region to hunt bison.

Taos Pueblo community

In order to survive, the Pueblo people had to adapt to changes in their environment. For example, they moved from Mesa Verde because changes in the climate made it difficult to farm. Once they settled near the Rio Grande, Zuni River, and Hopi mesas, they had to adapt again to these new environments. This is a major reason why each community developed a **unique** culture.

PUEBLO ORIGIN STORIES

CHAPTER 7

As you've learned, "Pueblo" is not one Native American nation, but a group of nations, so there are differences in their cultures. In fact, there are even cultural differences between clans within the same nation. This can be seen in Pueblo origin stories, which have spiritual qualities much like European religions. These origin stories were used to pass down knowledge of how Pueblo ancestors survived and adapted in their environment over thousands of years.

According to many Pueblo origin stories, ancestors of the Pueblo people lived underground, in a world below Earth. The stories tell of the people climbing out from a hole in the roof of the world below. In some accounts, they use a ladder or pine tree. In others, they climb through a hollow reed that was placed there by a being named Spider Grandmother. After arriving on Earth, the ancestors migrated and spread out throughout the land.

These elements of Pueblo origin stories can be seen in the way Ancestral Puebloans lived. Their original pit houses contained a sipapu, which was meant to represent the hole from which the first peoples emerged. Kivas—the underground ceremonial rooms—were entered through a hole in the roof. Some kivas contained a hole in the floor to represent the hole in the origin stories.

This photo shows carvings on stone that were created by the Hopi. It's likely the spiral circle and box in the center of the carving represent the hole where the Hopi believe their people entered Earth.

TRADITIONAL BELIEFS

CHAPTER 8

Traditionally, the Pueblo people believed in concepts that explained the relationship between people, nature, plants, and animals. Most Western Puebloans practiced a form of religion that involved kachinas, which are still important in modern Pueblo culture. Kachinas are spiritual beings that represent important aspects of Pueblo life, such as the sun, stars, corn, and animals. Kachinas can also represent the spirit of a **deceased** ancestor, a historical event, natural events, and ideas. In Pueblo culture, there are more than 500 different kachinas.

Kachinas are thought to have humanlike qualities. The Pueblo people believe kachinas can marry and have families. The kachinas are powerful, though they're not worshipped like gods would be. However, it's believed paying respect to kachinas will bring good fortune, such as rain or protection, to a community.

Kachinas are represented in traditional ceremonies by men who wear kachina masks.

The performer is said to have the kachina inside him while he participates in the ceremony. The Pueblo people also carve wooden dolls to represent kachinas. The dolls are given to Pueblo children as gifts and are used as a way to teach the children about the world and how their ancestors survived and adapted to their environment. Kachina masks and dolls are highly decorated.

This image, which was taken before 1900, shows Shongopavi Indians performing a **ritual** dance. The dancers are wearing kachina masks.

MEETING THE SPANISH

CHAPTER 9

Pueblo culture and lifestyle changed slowly over hundreds of years. However, no change was as great as that which came after the arrival of Europeans. The Pueblo people first encountered the Spanish in the 16th century. Spain claimed land in southwestern North America in 1539. In 1540, Spanish explorer Francisco Vázquez de Coronado arrived in Pueblo lands. The Spanish called the native people they found "pueblo," which is the Spanish word for "village," after the way their communities were organized.

Spanish influence threatened the survival of many Pueblo communities. The Spanish took over Pueblo lands, oppressing and killing anyone who stood in their way. They forced their religion and customs on the Puebloans and also brought over deadly diseases that killed thousands of Native Americans. Spanish **missionaries** burned kivas and sacred objects, including kachina masks. People who resisted were jailed, tortured, or killed.

In 1680, many Pueblo people, joined by Apache Indians, revolted against the Spanish. The revolt was led by a Pueblo **medicine man** who felt commanded by kachinas to bring back old ways of life. The Puebloans and Apache overthrew the Spanish, leaving 400 dead. The Pueblo people were free from Spanish rule for 12 years, until 1692.

The Pueblo Revolt was led by a San Juan Pueblo man named Po'Pay. He felt commanded by ancestral spirits in the form of kachinas to bring the old ways of life back to his people. Today, a statue of Po'Pay stands in the U.S. Capitol building.

FORCED CHANGE

CHAPTER 10

The Spanish returned to Pueblo lands in 1692 and once again took control of the area. Spanish influence had a great effect on Pueblo ways of life. The Spanish introduced horses and livestock, such as cattle and sheep. They brought new kinds of food to Pueblo lands, such as apples, melons, tomatoes, peppers, and wheat.

In 1848, this territory became part of the United States. The Pueblo people faced great challenges once again. The U.S. government forced Pueblo people to speak English and practice Christianity. They wanted the Pueblo people to adopt American customs and ways of life.

After the U.S. government took over territory in the Southwest, it claimed Pueblo land belonged to the United States, even though the Pueblo people had been there for hundreds of years. Treaties were signed that forced Pueblo men, women, and children onto **reservations**.

Pueblo children were especially affected by the U.S. government's harsh treatment. They were taken from their family and forced to attend boarding schools. They couldn't speak their own language, wear traditional clothing, or practice their own customs. This happened to many Native American children in North America.

This image was taken around 1870. It shows about 50 Native American children at a school on a reservation in Arizona.

THE PUEBLO TODAY

CHAPTER 11

Despite these hardships, the Pueblo people worked to hold on to their cultural identity. They adopted some new ways of life and managed to keep old traditions. They combined parts of both lifestyles into something new. For example, some of their religious ceremonies took on elements of Christianity.

In the 20th century, the U.S. government tried to right some of the wrongs it had committed against Native Americans. In 1934, Congress signed the Indian Reorganization Act, which protected Native Americans' rights. Today, many communities of Pueblo people are led by elected governors and tribal councils.

Today, there are more than 60,000 Pueblo people. There are 21 federally recognized Pueblo communities in the United States. Most are in New Mexico. The Hopi live in Arizona, and the Ysleta del Sur live in Texas.

Many Pueblo people today hold regular jobs. Many earn a living by making and selling traditional crafts, such as pottery, jewelry, and other forms of art. Pueblo people lead a modern lifestyle, but still celebrate their heritage through traditional ceremonies. Some ceremonies are open to nonnative people, which is an opportunity for people to learn about Pueblo culture.

This photo shows people performing the Eagle Dance, which is a ceremony that belongs to the San Juan Pueblo. The dance movements are meant to represent the way eagles fly and move.

FAMOUS PUEBLO PEOPLE

CHAPTER 12

Many successful people have come from Pueblo communities. Louis Tewanima, who was a Hopi man, won a silver medal in a running event at the 1912 Olympic Games. He set a U.S. running record that stood for 52 years. Juanita Suazo Dubray is a Taos woman who became famous for her pottery, which features designs important to the Pueblo culture, such as maize, lizards, and turtles. Pop Chalee, who was a woman of Taos

Pop Chalee

descent, was famous for her art and work in the radio and film industry. Nonnative artists have been inspired by the Pueblo culture, too. The Taos art colony in New Mexico was formed by artists attracted to the culture and geography that belongs to the Taos Pueblo.

Another famous Pueblo person is Leslie Marmon Silko, a Laguna Pueblo writer. She's known for writing about the relationship between the past and the present and how it has an effect on modern Pueblo life. Her most famous work, *Ceremony*, follows the story of a Laguna Pueblo man after he returns from war. The novel is known for the importance it places on Native American storytelling and traditions. Silko has won many awards for her writing.

Leslie Marmon Silko

The men and women mentioned in this chapter are just a few notable Pueblo people.

A UNIQUE CULTURE

CHAPTER 13

The story of Native Americans in the United States is one of hardship. Forced from their lands by European settlers, they were made to give up their traditional ways of life in favor of what nonnative people thought was best

for them. However, Native Americans worked to fight against these efforts and, in the process, have been able to hang on to the cultural heritage that's so important to them. The Pueblo people are part of this story.

Ancestors of some Pueblo peoples once lived in stone dwellings along cliffs. Ancestral Puebloans became successful farmers, excellent builders, and amazing artisans. These qualities followed the Pueblo people as they developed independent communities. Their traditions were shaped by their surroundings, and Puebloans worked to preserve them even as the Spanish and, later, the U.S. government tried to force the Pueblo people to give them up. Thanks to the efforts of Pueblo people in the past and present, their culture is still strong.

The Pueblo people live across many states and belong to many communities. However, their shared heritage has helped unite the thousands of Pueblo people who live in the United States today.

The Pueblo culture is kept alive through traditional ceremonies, which are performed throughout the year.

GLOSSARY

ancestor: A person who comes before others in their family tree.

anthropologist: A person who studies human cultures.

canteen: An object used for carrying and drinking water.

culture: The beliefs and ways of life of a group of people.

deceased: Dead.

environment: The surroundings in which a person, animal, or plant lives.

era: A long period of history known for particular features.

geometric: Having to do with repeated lines, angles, and curves.

heritage: Traditions that have been passed down from older generations.

medicine man: In Native American cultures, a person who is believed to have powers of healing and seeing into the future.

migration: The movement of people from one place to another.

missionary: A person sent to teach Christianity in another country.

origin story: A story that explains the creation of the world and the first people who lived in it.

reservation: Land set aside by the government for a specific Native American group or groups to live on.

ritual: A religious ceremony.

technique: A way of doing something.

unique: Being the only one of its kind.

FOR MORE INFORMATION

BOOKS

Cunningham, Kevin, and Peter Benoit. *The Pueblo*. New York, NY: Children's Press, 2011.

Cunningham, Kevin, and Peter Benoit. *The Zuni*. New York, NY: Children's Press, 2011.

Shea, Therese. *The Hopi People*. New York, NY: Gareth Stevens Publishing, 2015.

WEBSITES

Due to the changing nature of Internet links, PowerKids Press has developed an online list of websites related to the subject of this book. This site is updated regularly. Please use this link to access the list: www.powerkidslinks.com/sona/pueb

INDEX